THESE PEOPLE

The Wesleyan Poetry Program : Volume 103

THESE PEOPLE

LLOYD SCHWARTZ

Wesleyan University Press
Middletown, Connecticut

1/1982
Any Lit. Coll

Acknowledgment is gratefully made to the following periodicals in which these poems originally appeared: *American Review*, "Childhood," "Estelle's Testimony"; *Green House*, "Digger," "Interview," "Some Notes on My Father," "Song of the Self-Stimulator"; *The Massachusetts Review*, "Mental Cases"; *The New Republic*, "Self-Portrait"; *The New York Times* (Arts and Leisure), "78's"; *Partisan Review*, "On the Recent Deaths of His Friend Colonna and His Lady Laura," "The Wanderer"; *Ploughshares*, "Hannah," "Mug Shots," "The Recital," "Satie: Trois Mélodies," "Who's on First?"; *The Seattle Review*, "A Philosophical Problem"; *Seneca Review*, "Double Life," "Theocritus Schwartz"; *Shenandoah*, "Apparitions," "Interior Monologue".

ISBN 0-8195-1103-X (paper)
ISBN 0-8195-2103-5 (cloth)

Library of Congress Catalog Card Number: 81–13151

Manufactured in the United States of America
First Edition

CONTENTS

Childhood

In the imaginary kingdom of my only-childhood, I played all the parts—male and female, human and animal. "Lloyd" was the king of a world extending from the Royal Palace (home) to the far away island of the Unknown Castle, whose crystal stairways could be shattered, out of malevolence or ignorance, with a single touch.

There were eight "children"—four pairs of brothers and sisters, all cousins, the cousins of opposite sex nearest in age in love with each other.

They were gallant, beautiful, intelligent, and deeply moral. Their adventure was to protect the Unknown Castle from danger, advised and protected themselves by the animals, their only other friends.

This kingdom of my seven year old mind I kept entirely to myself.

●

We lived in my grandfather's house. He was my idol, though he had died years before I was born—well before the neighborhood had begun to turn slum. We had the only trees on the block.

We lived on the second floor of the three-story, shingled house, with its low green fence and curlicued iron gate. An alley went back the whole length of the house to a garage—with a great skylight—converted from my grandfather's stable when there were no more horses. Seven or eight cars rented it.

He was a harness-maker. He came here from Russia just before the turn of the century. But he didn't like America, and went to England, then to the war in South Africa—to harness English horses.

When his brothers bought a farm in Massachusetts, he came back. My grandmother and their five children were still in Russia. He finally sent for them, after a fire burned down the whole town; my mother was three.

His brothers left the farm; my oldest aunt got married. He went to New York, found a house and stable in Brooklyn; came back, sold the farm; and this time with the whole family, for the last time, moved again.

Mustachioed, barrel-chested, he had sad round eyes, and a beautiful voice. Everyone said he loved to sing. His name was Singer, how could he not love to sing?

> *In the fireplace*
> *A little fire's burning*
> *Warm the house must be*
>
> *And the little rabbi*
> *With his little children*
> *Learn their ABC*

.

Every day our next-door neighbor's granddaughter came with her mother to visit. I loved her. I gave my favorite "child" her name.

We played. Sometimes "Hiding O'Seek" in back of the house; or "Three Musketeers"—all of us tearing out of the alley yelling

"Dar-TANYON!"

Or sometimes, with some of the older children, "Dare"—e.g., sneaking up to the door of the hunchbacked and hooknosed old lady on the other side of the alley, who didn't speak a word of English (it was my fearful duty to light her gas-range on Friday nights), and singing

> *Old Mother Witch*
> *Stepped in a ditch*
> *Picked up a penny and thought she was rich!*

then running for our lives.

Once we were playing with a boy from across the street, and (I wasn't thinking) I started to talk to Tiger; who, unselfconsciously, answered. The princess with my favorite name and her brother were there too— talking.

Suddenly it hit me that it was *me* talking, talking with a girl's voice—; pretending to be an animal—; in front of *other people*.

I had betrayed myself, and my whole kingdom.

They didn't say anything or laugh. Effortlessly (as crystal stairways, or shingled houses, skylights, gates, trees, grandfathers—or childhoods— give way to a touch),

they had begun another game.

8

Who's on First?

"You can be so inconsiderate."

"You are too sensitive."

"Then why don't you take my feelings into consideration?"

"If you weren't so sensitive it wouldn't matter."

•

"You seem to really care about me only when you want me to do something for you."

"You do too much for people."

•

"I thought you were going home because you were too tired to go with me to a bar."

"I was. But Norman didn't want to come here alone."

•

"I'm awfully tired. Do you mind taking the subway home?"

(*Silence.*)

"You could stay over . . . "

(*Silence.*)

"I'll take you home."

(*Silence.*)

•

"Why do we have sex only when you want to?"

"Because you want to have sex all the time."

•

"Relationships work when two people equally desire to give to each other."

"Relationships rarely work."

•

"Do you love me?"

"Of course—; but I resent it."

•

"Why aren't you more affectionate?"

"I am."

•

"Couldn't we ever speak to each other without irony?"

"Sure."

•

"I love you, you know."

"Yes . . . but why?"

•

"Do you resent my advice?"

"Yes. Especially because you're usually right."

•

"Why do you like these paintings?"

"What isn't there is more important than what is."

•

"Your taste sometimes seems strange to me."

"I'm a Philistine."

"A real Philistine would never admit it."

"I suppose you're right."

•

"Aren't you interested in what I care about?"

"Yes. But not now."

•

"We should be more open with each other."

"Yes."

"Shall we talk things over?"

"What is there to say?"

•

"Are you ever going to cut down on your smoking?"

"It's all right— I don't inhale."

•

"Sometimes I get very annoyed with you."

"The world is annoying."

•

"Your cynicism is too easy."

"Words interfere with the expression of complex realities."

•

"Do you enjoy suffering?"

"You can't work if you don't suffer."

"But we suffer anyway."

"I know."

•

"Do you think we ever learn anything?"

"I've learned to do without."

•

"You're always so negative."

"I feel death all the time."

"Are you afraid of anything?"

"Not working."

•

"What shall we do for dinner?"

"It doesn't matter—whatever you'd like."

•

"Why don't you care more?"

"I do."

Mug Shots

"In business you have to know *people* . . . Try selling
frozen pizza in the North End—it's like shoveling
shit against the tide; the more 'ethnic' the neighborhood,
the more they like to start from scratch. Everything fresh!

Wait a generation, they'll change . . . Then, move in."

        •

"Are you saying it was a conspiracy?
The CIA?"
        "Not CIA—*KKK!* The killers had
their initials, King and the Kennedys:
KK&K . . . Working hand in glove with
the big 'M' of course.
        Money and racism,
what else is there? *That's* the conspiracy.

The biggest cover-up wasn't Watergate,
it was the Warren Commission: 'WC'—
a shithouse.
        Now they're trying to lay it
all on Cuba . . . I don't think the CIA knew
anything about it (until after it was over,
of course).
        At least, I'm not sure they
thought it would really happen. They're
not James Bond!

Look—*Oswald*; then *Ruby*; now that German guy
who 'committed suicide.'
        Coincidence? Come on!
People don't want to believe what's
right in front of them.
        Look at Nixon on TV. How
could anyone swallow that? Didn't you get even
a little suspicious? I bet 'Bebe-gun' Rebozo
masterminded the assassination!"

"King too?"
"It's *economics*—property values; job security.
If you're poor, KEEP OUT.
                              Rich blacks rub it in.

There's only *victims* and *criminals* . . .

'Protect' yourself from anyone who wants
what you have—
                    or hire someone.
People didn't go to 'The Godfather' for
Marlon Brando; they shelled out to see
the World's Best Insurance Company in action.

Forget gun control, my friend; we love
sharpshooters—we let them get away with murder."

                    •

"Black?"
        "Yes."
                "How many?"
                            "Three."
                                    "How old?"
"Young—twenties. Big guys."
                            "Call that
young? They've been out on the streets for
years, probably. Did they show a weapon?"

"No, just surrounded me. They were coming
down the other side of the street while I was
getting out of my car, and suddenly—
I'm surrounded. Tore my pants pocket right off!"

"You were lucky. Some guys get cut up . . .
pretty bad."
            "Lucky I didn't have much on me."

"Guy with his girlfriend in the park, sleeping
peacefully in the sun—people all around. Wakes up,
there's a knife up against his throat.

Guy wants money for drugs, says: 'Don't move,
or I'll slit your fuckin' throat. I want every-
thing you got—*I don't care what happens to me.*'

He'da been dead before anyone could've helped.

. . . Think you could spot one?"

He pulls out three photo albums. The pictures
look like the ones you get in a booth for a
quarter, only bigger.
                      All the same poses—
full face; profile. Ten or twelve to a page.

Hundreds of pages.

More "real" than a high school yearbook, or
family album . . . The pictures
don't run together. The identical poses
exaggerate the idiosyncrasies:

faces round, or sunken; hair slicked down,
or fuzzy, or limp; skin very dark, or
almost white . . .
                      One has an earring and a
blond wig; one has hardly any teeth; one has
a long, deep scar.
                      A lot aren't wearing shirts . . .
Naked? Dangerous?

"You can stop when you get tired."

Their expressions are unusually clear:
scared, or cynical; alert, or spaced out.
One looks ashamed; another is crying;
one's grinning.
                      One looks "intelligent."

—Which ones are guilty?

They all look tired . . . and guilty.

I close the book. A thin young man comes in.
"White or black?" "Black." "How old?" "Early teens."
They hand him a set of albums. I start to leave.

"Any weapons?" "A knife . . . They pulled a knife on me."
I reach into my pocket. No weapon; only
keys. Is my car still there?

I get up. I feel dizzy, and numb; my eyes ache.
—In an album I hadn't noticed, I see

my picture . . .

full face, profile; black and white.
I look nervous, "intelligent," ashamed;
I'm not wearing a shirt . . .

Shoplifting? tax evasion? defamation of character?
reckless driving? disturbing the peace? possession of
narcotics? indecent exposure? fraud?

It's too dark to see.

—I go out; it's daylight. I look around; the street
is empty . . . I walk to my car,
looking both ways, before I cross the street.

Hannah

I walk on hooked rugs; my beds are covered with
patchwork. Across the road they sell
corn and red beans—fresh picked,
and the milk in bottles has a layer of cream
an inch thick at the top. This was my father's home
I have come back to. My elderly cousin
is working her latest jig-saw puzzle in the spare room.
My guest for the weekend is a young teacher,
with hair longer than mine, and a nicely trimmed
beard; he is reading my first editions.
We'll talk about novels and politics, read the papers,
play Scrabble with my elderly cousin, catch up on
the unread magazines. He'll help me carry and unload
the books I have moved here from the city; steel-wool
the old chest, ready for refinishing.
So many complicated, trivial, and
lovely things. A sturdy old leather bible, with gold edges,
and patterns in the rough grain, the names of ancestors
firmly inscribed. I have had a good life,
without sex, or sordidness, or unmerited happiness.

Estelle's Testimony

They said I was "promiscuous"
(did I get it right?)—that means
sleeping around? Well, I am,
and why not? I don't
take money or anything; I just like
sex, and being sexy.
                    It's pretty standard
most of the time. I did meet a guy once
who wanted me to hit his thing with a
leather belt, and call him names. It wasn't bad,
but who needs it? I guess
I'm kind of conservative . . . just
a guy on top, strong
and hard.

I hope you don't think I'm trying to be
vulgar—but you wanted the honest T,
and that's it.

Once a guy who picked me up in the movies
handed me a ten dollar bill, after I went up
to his place—
                I nearly cried.

Sometimes I think of making it
with another chick; but that's weird:
just fingers—you might as well
do it yourself . . .

But I really dig people. I like to
communicate, to get close to a person.
That's why I liked Arthur, I could feel
close to him—
                never mind the age difference;
I mean we really had something going.

I know it sounds funny, but I
wasn't even that interested in his dough.

He was different, you know what I mean?
More distinguished—
                    older, I guess, but
not just; something about his white hair—
I just loved to see my fingers
running through it.
                    He was a very sexy man.

He loved to touch me: sometimes in my sleep
I would feel him,
                    very softly moving his palms
back and forth, over my boobs. I wouldn't wake up,
but it was nice . . .

We never went all the way, until that last time.
I would've let him,
but he couldn't do it—
I think he was afraid of his heart.

It's funny though, that last time
I didn't really want to.
                    It's like it was
so special. I mean I've never really
just *slept* with a guy.
It was like he was my father or something.

And that night, we went for dinner—he took me
to this really posh place. And I of course got
kind of plastered; and we
danced . . .
                    And like usual, I went
back to his place.

I undressed, and got into bed as usual;
and I felt so good—I just sat up, and
while he was taking off his shoe
I hugged him,
                    and kissed his forehead . . .
And he got so turned on, he practically
jumped on top of me. Christ! he still

had his shirt on, and one shoe—and he was really
hard—
I've never seen him get hard before.

I don't know, I suddenly felt so ashamed.
I wanted him to stop, and I said
"Arthur, please, please stop" and he wouldn't.
I think he really wanted to come,
—it must have been so many years;

and he couldn't.

And then he stopped, very sudden. And
that was it.

I felt so sick, I just had to get out of there. He was
still in me,
so I pushed him off.
I knew he was dead.
I got dressed, and I started to leave,
but I see his wad of bills on the dresser, and
without thinking, I took it.
Then
I remembered his ring—a kind of snake ring,
with a diamond in its eye; I always
liked it a lot . . .

I didn't want him to die.
I only wanted it for a souvenir.
Nobody ever did it to me
and died.

Interview

"I thought once I'd like to be a kleptomaniac,
—but in reverse: give everything away.
Sneak into a store, pockets
full, jacket bulging
with my belongings; and discreetly slip them
onto shelves, behind counters. Imagine everyone
doing this? Storerooms filled; warehouses
overflowing . . . "

—Wouldn't that imply psychological liberation from material possession
at the expense of economic ruin?

"Pure fantasizing on my part."

—How have you lived?

"I freaked out after the divorce.
Took the car, a credit card, and
eleven dollars—drove to Virginia; Maine; New York;
in that order. Finally saw a doctor,
who gave me sleeping pills, which I took
all at once—in a parking lot of a shopping center,
late at night.
But someone found me. I was
'rescued.' And 'rested.' When I got out,
I didn't even want to see the children—didn't see them
for three months. Now they come
every other weekend."

—And since the divorce?

"I ran into a high school friend,
whom I hadn't seen for fifteen years. He
introduced me to his sister-in-law
(he's divorced now), and we just hit it right.
We were lovers until I met
David, and then
I wanted him more than her.

It was hard for her to understand.
I see her often; we are not
lovers; but it's not over yet.
David and I aren't lovers
anymore now—I feel more paternal; but
it's not over yet, either."

—Very interesting. But I really meant to ask
how your life has changed.

"I was straight, domestic, professional.
All my friends were 'professional.' We
sometimes had poets to dinner. I am no longer a
home-owner, architect, or husband;
not even employed.
I let my hair grow. I've stopped being
'adult.' I think I've started to grow up."

—What about me?

"We are only a beginning. I love you
sometimes. You will have to be patient.
It's not over yet."

Satie: Trois Mélodies

The Bronze Statue   (Léon-Paul Fargue)

The frog on the tumbler-game in the park
Gets bored at night, when it all gets dark.
She thinks a statue's life is absurd,
Always about to pronounce a great word,
                                        The Word . . .

She would rather be—as she'd often hope—
Blowing bubbles of music with moonlight soap
Like the others.
                        The gilded wash-house nearby
Shines through the branches, like coins in the sky . . .
In the heart of the day they throw pieces of money;
Which she cannot eat (which she doesn't think funny).
The echoing coins fill the cabinets
Of her numbered pedestal . . . But she soon forgets.
The sleepy insects, after all their play,
Fall asleep in her mouth with the fall of each day.

Dapheneo   (M. God)

—Explain, Dapheneo.
Tell me what you call this tree whose fruits are little crying birds.

—Oh, this tree, Chrysaline,
Is just a tear tree.

—Oh. I thought pear trees were the trees that always gave us pears,
Dapheneo.

—Yes, Chrysaline.
Pear trees always give us pears,
But tear trees are the trees that give us little crying birds.

—Oh.

The Mad Hatter   (René Chalupt)

Astonished to establish, is the Hatter,
    That his pocket-watch is three days slow—
For he greased it with the very best butter;
    But breadcrumbs fell into the works, and he
    Immersed the watch totally in tea . . .
That won't make it work any better.

Digger

"Would you believe I went to college? Yeah,
I majored in philosophy. No shit;
for one year. Man I guess I should've stayed.
But who can tell? I never figured I'd
wind up like this. (I usually don't
say much; it's funny to be talking.)
                                  So
I came back home. Bartended. A gay place,
couple of others—Boston, Cambridge; then
I got to know Jimmy. The two of us
wanted to open our own bar. *The Den*
was being sold. We came up with some cash;
man, it was ours! Plenty of hassles
with permits, cops, mortgages, licenses—
but we made it work. Cleaned it up, hired
a band for weekends. Man it was a blast.
Chicks, bikes, dope, booze—man, money . . . everything.

It was unreal, like things would all work out.

But Jimmy threw me out for shooting up.
Then we got framed on this bad-ass coke deal.
Man we got really framed bad. Jimmy's fault;
brings home a guy he just meets in the bar,
—narcs, cops, guns, chicks; took us by surprise.
I never figured I'd wind up with four
years minimum in the federal pen."

I liked him when I met him. A kind of boyish
openness balanced the leather, bracelets, and bikes
pulling in at 4, or out at 7 A.M.
Music blasting up through the floor. Loud
parties. Beer and dope. Just beer and dope . . .

And girls—a constant stream—though only
one kept coming back, tougher than him,
even after trying to kill herself—

threatening to kill the girl next door
she thought was sleeping with him . . . the last straw.

Two things, though, I find hardest to forgive—
my ex-girl sleeping with him, a floor away
from where we lived together for two years;
and Humphrey, his Saint Bernard, left out on the back porch
while he was gone for a week.

                        "—took us by surprise.
I never figured I'd wind up with four
years minimum in the federal pen;

I'm shaking . . . man I guess I'm really scared."

A *Philosophical Problem*

"Hello?"
          "Oh, hi."

"I'm sorry, did I wake you?"
                              "No, but I
can't talk now . . . There's someone here."

"I'm sorry. I'd like to talk to you. Can I
call you back later?"
                         "I . . . I don't think so.
Let me call you tomorrow."

"All right . . . all right. I'm afraid I've
done something foolish."
                          "Let's
talk about it tomorrow. I'll call you. G'night."

"Good night."

Please don't be upset. I feel fine today.
Really. I'd like to explain to you
what happened last night.
I had to *hurt* myself. Can you understand?
Not kill myself. I knew almost three years ago
I would do this, sooner or later.
The analysts don't help you—
they only teach you how to play.
Of *course* it's my mother's fault
for not wanting to touch me;
for divorcing my father; for
neither of them wanting to take me . . .
How could I *not* feel worthless?
How could I justify my existing?

But how can anyone—
whatever their parents were like? My problem

was not psychological; it is philosophical.
What right has *anyone* to be here?

Of course I lied to my analyst—I told her
I was depressed. She said you
can't *make* people love you;
you can't make someone even like you . . .
I've learned. I tried
not to tell you how much I cared, not to
force myself on you; and then I had to . . .

But all along, I had the feeling that only
pain—actual, physical pain—
would relieve my depression.

Of course, you told me I
didn't love you. How could I
when we knew each other so little?
when our "encounters" were so unsuccessful,
especially for me . . . It was true.
But I didn't believe you. I admit, now I can see
you were right: it wasn't you,
but my conviction, my fantasy
of our endless, undiluted bliss . . . You say
it could have been anyone—
if *you* were not the first person I met here,
I would have latched on to someone else.
I'm sorry it was you.
—I won't bother you again. I don't even
want to see you now; frankly,
I don't even like you anymore . . .

Maybe this still sounds crazy, but I think
if you—or someone—could have
only *touched* me last night (I don't mean sex, just
some physical contact),
I don't think I would have done it.

I hope this doesn't sound like

blackmail. Believe me, I don't mean it to!
I do know what I need.
And I was sure I wouldn't kill myself . . .

All week I felt driven. I went
to a concert alone
and couldn't stand being stuck in my seat.
I was even rude to another friend who
insisted I go with him for a drink . . . And then
running into you last night, and your sweet offer
to drive me to the subway; and your look
of *boredom*
when I finally told you how I felt about you—;
I panicked. I went straight home and took
three sleeping pills, and a glass of wine.
It only got worse; I
couldn't get the panic out of my system.

It was not crazy—though you'll probably
think it was; I knew
just what I needed to do . . . I used a pair
of very blunt scissors;
a two-by-four would have been sharper.
I knew I wouldn't kill myself.
It was very messy. I'm sorry;
but it worked . . . I knew it would work.

Song of the Self-Stimulator

Johnny had a steamboat
The steamboat had a bell
The steamboat went to Heaven
       And Johnny went to

I have a lover
My lover treats me well
A very fine lover
       But I love to masturbate

It makes me feel guilty
It makes me feel swell
I must like feeling guilty
       And I like to masturbate

I do it whenever I want to
I do it whenever I can
I don't care why I want to
       I just masturbate

Sometimes I look at pictures
Sometimes I close my eyes
They're very fine pictures
       That you need to masturbate

Sometimes in public places
Sometimes alone in my bed
You can be seen in public places
       And they watch you masturbate

Sometimes I do it just once
Sometimes until I get sore
It's more real more than once
       When you really masturbate

No one else can really hurt you
You're doing it yourself

No one can come between you
    When you want to masturbate

Oh, I'd like to get married
Oh, I'd like to have kids
But why should I get married
    While I can masturbate?

Take it nice and easy
Make it good and hard
Too hard, too easy
    That's how you masturbate

Let it come slowly
Stretch it as long as you can
It doesn't matter how slowly
    Everything waits while you masturbate

First thing in the morning
After every meal
Each evening, every morning
    Trying to masturbate—

Shake it: shake the hand
That holds my toothbrush and my pen
This hand—the very hand
    I use to masturbate

Johnny had a steamboat
The steamboat had a bell
The steamboat went to Heaven
    And Johnny went to

Hell-o Operator
Give me Number Nine
If the party doesn't answer
    Give me back my dime

Double Life

My father was a fundamentalist minister.
He sent me to a Baptist college, to become
a fundamentalist minister. I met Kathy there;
her father was a fundamentalist minister.

We were so innocent, we wanted
what our parents wanted—
                              I never felt
I had pleased my father before.

I got my degree—and a parish. Kathy
was going to have a baby. I was twenty-three;
everything was perfect;
and I started going to pieces . . .

When Kathy was in the hospital I began to feel
all alone, frightened—though occasionally,
oddly exhilarated by my confusion.
Every day I would wander around the city.

Once I passed the bus station, where
a guy, my age, smiled at me
as I went by . . . I smiled back—somehow
reassured that I existed.

I walked by, turned around (he smiled
again), continued.
He followed me; I stopped. He said hello,
and we started to talk.

The weather led to God, and
to his room. We had a drink, and he came
and sat down next to me. He leaned over
and rested his hand on my thigh.

Then he kissed me on the mouth—his tongue
reaching all the way in.
He started to undress me—I
let him. He took me to bed and we "made love."

At that exact moment my first son was born.

                    •   •   •

It wasn't the last time that happened . . .

I liked it. I found men, even the most
money-grubbing hustlers, in some ways more
responsive, more intuitively understanding,
than Kathy. I was brought up to think it was

degrading to go to a prostitute,
but I looked for hustlers
as soon as I learned where they could be found.
The embarrassment I felt, literally

stumbling into my first, my very first,
bar—of any kind! I was surely
degrading myself;
                    damning myself . . .

But the more "wrong things" I
kept doing, the more I realized
how little everything else I had done
ever meant to me—; how little

I ever thought about my life.

It would be intolerable not to leave the Church.
I'm still afraid to tell Kathy. But I've
got to. I can't live with her
unless I tell her everything—; soon.

A double life?
                    Two halves
of one life,
not touching . . .

I've got to begin to think about myself.

Some Notes on My Father

Maybe he was happy in Paris. He remembers a few French words, considers himself an expert. (He escaped from Roumania to avoid being drafted; got as far as Paris.) When I was fourteen, my aunt hinted that I might have a nice "little sister" running around someplace in France: "She'd be in her forties by now."

What made me feel ashamed at fourteen, is currently fashionable, even respectable.

Do I *admire* now, what for so many years I regarded—in him—as cowardice, escapism, and immorality?

"You should forgive him . . . try! Maybe when you are older."

•

He worked in sweatshops; I have a photograph. He's wearing (like the others) a vest and tie; half sitting on the edge of his sewing table, way in the back.

Energy and dignity frustrated by poverty and contempt.

His boss stands with his arms folded, a cigarette
dangling.

"Anti-Semite, he should be buried in his mother's grave."

•

I never learned the details. My mother told me he had been divorced—in 1940, the year they were married. He must have been over forty by then; he changed his age so many times (immigration, employment, un-employment), he never knew for sure how old he was.

He can't remember now whether or not he had actually married his first wife.

•

He'd yell at me to get off the phone, to turn out the light, to stop spending his money.

He was the "mean old man" of the block. He terrified the kids whose softball got batted into our yard:

GET OUT OF HERE FROM HERE
SONOFABITCH!
YOU WANT I SHOULD CALL THE POLICE?

He could be heard at the ends of the block calling me "Crazy Professor," and "Crazy BASTARD."

I told him *he* was the crazy one, and provoked him into swinging the open blade of a hedge-clipper at my head. It hit my elbow . . .

I didn't speak a single word to him for two years, before I left home. (Somewhere I've preserved in a drawer a hanky with a stiff, brown bloodstain.)

"*I* yelled? When did I yell?"

•

When anyone visits, he tells them how "Niggers," "Portarickens," Unions, Nixon, the Kennedys, Roosevelt, Stalin, La Guardia, the Italians, the Irish, the Germans, the Russians, other Jews, and the neighbors

are all no damn good.

•

There's too much furniture, too many plants, too much junk on the shelves, too many bad pictures on the walls.

This year he repainted the garage door and "rearranged" my old room. He insisted, as always, that my mother watch him work.

I'm trying to learn not to be "better" at what I hate him for doing.

Sometimes when I come "home," I bring clothes for him to fix, to make him feel useful. I ask his permission to use the phone, to avoid arguments (my mother's suggestion). Sometimes it works. My mother hasn't quite given up.

He sits in his reclining chair with "my" dog in his lap (eighteen years old and totally blind—too old to be put away).

He complains of his stomach, his eyes, his back, his head . . .

He has no recollection of having ever hurt anyone.

Theocritus Schwartz

"Theo" . . .
            no one would have to know his real name—

with its wish for better days,
where life may not have been easy, but was
easier to live . . .

and everyone, and
every thing,
was diminished by a death;

and poetry seems to have been
as natural as singing, or dying.

And "Theo"
has a kind of rough-and-ready sound, yet still
intelligent—

"Lloyd" was too delicate for a "Schwartz,"
too embarrassingly little like
other names in Brooklyn in the '40s—

forcing me to
fight, or find protection,
or hide;

children seem to me some kind of monster.

Yet a few are also
people—distinct; challenging;
charming . . .

But dangerous: the *art nouveau* glass
stuck in the highest cupboard,
to emerge into the light of day only
decades later.

And inconvenient: giving up the concert, because

the babysitter had some
last minute homework,—or was afraid
of getting raped on her way from the bus.

But worst, the worry . . .

My mother worried,
though still has the good sense
to let me go my own way—;

I would worry, and
wouldn't—;

I would worry he was doing
what I didn't.
Or did.
Or what I fought to do.

I would be *responsible* (possessive);
affectionate (jealous);
demanding attention and affection (like my father),
—a repository for wisdom and information.

And risking hostility (which my father and I
shared for so many years).
And indifference
(which he faces in me now).

And judgment.

How do parents *bear* it?

—Giving a name;
captivating an audience; guaranteeing
remembrance . . .
        My son as Masterpiece.

Theocritus, Theo—is it fear
or wisdom,
that insists on your delay?

78's

for Frank Bidart

Breakable; heavy; clumsy; the end of a side
the middle of a movement—or phrase
(the faults are obvious); surface noise;
one opera—three albums, four inches, thirty-three sides wide . . .

But under the noise, the surface, the elegant
labels, the bright shellac—Revolutions: Szigeti,
Schnabel, Busch, Beecham, Casals, Toscanini (*new '30s disk star at
sixty*);

all their overtones—understood, amplified, at hand:

Our Masters' Voices taking our breath,
revelations per minute, winding up in a living
room—turning the tables, taking off—moving: moving
faster (they make us think) than the speed of death.

Interior Monologue

These rooms . . .
                      If I could see them again
for the first time—

Dark blue dining room, with varnished,
dark brown, built-in wooden cupboards (space
for books); fleurs-de-lys in the bedroom,
perfume bottles on the bathroom
wallpaper, wallpaper in the other rooms
nondescript, shot through with gold—
faded rectangles where pictures were hung, the outline
of a huge cruciform in the bedroom . . .
                                      Imagining I can
                                      see them now
for the first time . . .

I like them—;
                      though I prefer flat white,
a blank tablet.

Gas fireplace, 1910? 1920? Wainscoting
in the kitchen. A back porch! Four rooms
circling a hallway—the phone could reach
into every room . . .

(Mattress on the bedroom floor. A huge chair
where I could throw my clothes. My desk
right between those windows. Pictures
clashing with the wallpaper . . .)

Front door looks like someone tried to break in.
(Piano in the dining room. Speakers
in the living room.) Closets,
outlets . . .

—Could I share it?
                      It would be hard; too cramped
for two.

Where would I put my records?
                    Could we afford a place
big enough for both of us?
Could we *ever* find one big enough? . . .

I'd hate to have to move . . .
Where would I put my books?
I don't want to live alone.

" . . . I'll take it!"

The Wanderer

I'm talking about what isn't there anymore,
the *past*—"Ultimate Nostalgia"—a dead end.

I had two friends. Married. I thought they were
my best friends—the both of them; for five,
six years.
        And I don't know, they didn't call
me, I didn't call them . . . It's been since February—
over three months. I can't even tell them
I'm leaving; what's the use?
                Maybe I'll
write to them. Maybe I'll call them
when I come back,—*if* I come back.
                   I'm starting
to get too attached to city life anyway!
It's no good to be dependent on *anything*,
even a city . . .
        "CONSTRUCTIVE NIHILISM."

I think I'm getting cynical!
              But what happened?
We *liked* each other. Maybe we liked each other
too much; maybe they got scared . . .
               I thought
six years would make us "inseparable." I guess
we didn't know each other as much as we thought.

—Maybe I'm too romantic.
            Why else would
I be going out into the woods?
           The only thing
I'm going to worry about now is if there's enough
room in my pack for my books . . .

           You know what
I'm taking? Whitman, Baudelaire, and the
Arabian Nights,—right?

Whitman is for
wandering—or sitting by the ocean,
in my tent, reading "Out of the Cradle
Endlessly Rocking." And every night, one
of the *Arabian Nights* . . .
                              Baudelaire is probably
too much; that's the first book I leave behind.

—I'm planning to shed my possessions as I go.
That's *all* I'm planning.
                              I have three shirts,
four pairs of socks . . . that's one pair too many,
but I suppose you can't throw good clothes away.

Possessions are ridiculous!
                              It's what I'm
trying to get away from . . .
                              and even now,
I can't: I've got this *tent*, and this *knife*,
and this fucking *backpack*, where I have to keep
my fucking *underwear*—
                              there's no escape.

But anything will be better than this city,
which I don't even want to remember;
—which is going to explode any second,
anyway . . . I don't want to be around to
hear it.
          I'm an Anarchist,—but I'm
a *socialist* Anarchist: Socialist;
Anarchist; Existentialist . . .
                              It makes sense.
Think about it: *Existentialism*
is what you believe; *Anarchy* is what
you do, right? We're all *alone*, right? And we act
alone.
          But you can still do things for
other people—that's where the *Socialism*
comes in. It makes sense!

But I don't know . . . I'm
not sure *what* I believe anymore. All I know is
I talk too much;
                    —and I've got to get away.

I feel nervous about going. I've never done
anything so completely on my own . . .
                              I'm nervous
about hitching, too. What if the cops
pick me up with this grass on me? I've heard
of guys being stripped by some sadist cop
who shoves his hand under your balls, or
up your ass, looking for—god knows what—"Illegal
Stimulants."
                    Maybe I should get rid of
the grass.
                    But the whole point is to be
in my tent—*mellow*—by the sea, reading
"Out of the Cradle Endlessly Rocking."
High Noon—any time of the day! A little
loving, a little smoke, some good words . . .

I believe in loving,
                    not *love*—"The Golden Chain."
Listen, my mother just left my father
after twenty-eight years, and still lives
in the same apartment house.
                              Why did she split?
Why bother? They never talked to each other
anyway. None of us ever talked.
I was pretty close with my father, but
we never *said* anything.
                    I have four
brothers, and they're all a little crazy;
—look at *me*!
                    It's not a coincidence.

"The Bonds of Matrimony" . . . I hope
I never have to get married.

                                        —See this?
I can't even remember where I got it.
It's gold. Someone gave it to me . . .
                                        I guess
I remember. It was a guy who liked me—
he made it. A hippie goldsmith . . . I liked
him, too.
            It couldn't have worked; he wanted
to live with me . . .
                        I'm going to give it to my
first future infatuation, the first new girl
I leave: "My darling (what was your name?), this
is for you to remember me by . . . So long!"

Nothing to lose but my chain!
                                    —One less to carry.

I could write a good poem about that;
or a *novel* . . . MY LIFE & LOVES.
                                    You know that poem,
"They flee from me who sometimes did me seek"?
—Sir Thomas Wyatt. He knew what he was
talking about.
                Or maybe *I flee from them* . . .
Both; it's about the same.
                            Or Shakespeare: "Farewell,
thou art too dear for my possessing . . ."
                                    They knew.

I don't think a good poem has been written
in a hundred years.
                        What the hell do I care
about some broad's period? or some guy's
fucking hard-on? All these fucking ego trips
and masturbation fantasies.
                            Or else
anemic iambic pentameter academic
exercises. No one—NO ONE—writes
about important things anymore.

                                    Rimbaud
did, Whitman did. Where's the Socialist-
Anarchist-Existentialist *POET?*

—I'm working on it; but I'm not there yet.

I've been writing a lot . . .
                              I always write things down;
I write *everything* down: look at these notebooks.
I kept a diary for about three years . . .
                                          I'm
trying to talk myself into leaving it.
There's no room;—why should I take it with me?
I keep re-reading it, to see if I can
find out where things went wrong: it doesn't help.

I hate my poems. They sound phony; and they
don't make sense.
                    I know what I want to say—
but it never comes out right; the words all
get stuck somewhere in my head.
                                  I know they're
in there; why is it so hard to find
the right ones?
                  That's another reason to
keep moving . . . I'm bound to learn *something.*

I should call a couple of people before I leave.
A girl I worked with, a guy I met in a bar
a few months ago—we were pretty friendly;
smoked a lot . . .
                    I hate goodbyes. That's one
of the problems about leaving—they're too
easy to say; you find out how little
you feel.
            I think I won't.
                              Right now
I feel like I'm not anywhere . . . except
still maybe a little too close to home.

Mental Cases

"—And the second is like unto it, Thou shalt love
thy neighbor as thyself . . . " In the middle of

our Passion Play, a thin, run-down young man—in a rage—
runs down the aisle, jumps onto the stage

shouting: "You *bastards*, you have NO RIGHT!"
and stands there with an open razor, ready to fight.

He jabs the air with the blade. He twists
around; we flinch. He waits . . . Then he slashes his wrists.

Nobody moves. Blood starts dripping down his hands—soaking
his dirty shirt; I feel like I'm choking.

Jesus sneaks up behind him and grabs the blade; awkwardly,
we grab him—try to drag him off. He

struggles; we hang on—the audience
applauds! . . . He starts to rave about our "ungodly offense."

Someone phones the police. We get him into a chair,
and finally, he stops resisting; his mind seems elsewhere.

He starts to sob: "I want to, I want to confess
my sins . . ." Then cooler—almost *affable* (and bleeding less),

he shows us manifestations
of several previous self-mutilations.

The police arrive; he goes quietly away
with them. Relieved, but shaking, we go back to the play,

throwing ourselves into the Crucifixion
with more than usual conviction.

Next day he's back—free.
He's "OK now," he says. "Sometime I'd like to see

the rest of the show." He's only come to find
some pamphlets and magazines he'd left. "You didn't mind,

did you?" he asks wearily. "So far, the only
one I've ever hurt—is me."

He goes; "*See* ya!" he waves. That night we're all distracted;
it's days before the play is better acted.

2

The sun was shining on the sea,
shining with all its might;
waves of clouds were breaking
delicately over the sky-blue sky.

Meredith giggled: "You're gonna *love* this!"

The clouds began to shape themselves
into fingers—pointing; then curling
suggestively.

"Do you *see* what the clouds are doing?"

Meredith was amused by my inexperience; I
caught on—it was "good stuff."

All at once, I was in a familiar amusement park;
not a real one,—a black-and-white murder mystery
side-show, with a grotesque mechanical fortune teller,
rocking from side to side, and leering darkly
through her glass booth.
                              A roller coaster
rushed by: P-O-W!
                    W-H-O-O-S-H!
                                    H-E-L-P!

I saw the words—even the exclamations—
written out;
              flashing, in broad red letters,
across the silent carnival.

My head was spinning. I seemed to be
at the wrong end of a tunnel. I could see the beach
through a tiny opening
                              way in the distance . . .
But the harder I kept trying
to reach it, the further away it got.
                                        I saw
Meredith lying next to me, on the beach—;
but my mind was stuck
                          in the literally endless tunnel.

I tried to concentrate on Meredith. But she was
covered with blood—; everyone on the beach was
covered with blood . . .
                        I couldn't look;
nothing *made sense*; everything was *coming apart*—

ISOLATION. CORRUPTION. DISSOLUTION . . .

What else *was* there?
                        Suddenly I understood EVERYTHING.

When I looked up, five wavy clouds were
slowly circling each other, as in a trick lens;
I said to myself: "It's the drug."
                              I could
barely hear the sound of my own voice.

Then I was back at the carnival . . .
the sinister fortune teller in the shadow of
the towering roller coaster; the comic strip words;
the terrifying tunnel—
                        would I ever get out?
Could anyone ever find me?
                              There was Meredith
in the distance, covered with blood—;
there was no way out.
                        I understood it all.

Overhead, the clear blue sky kept unravelling

its sexy clouds. Meredith was next to me,
giggling. There was nothing to be afraid of.

But I kept thinking: these "visions"—
why should they be like everyone else's?
What did they have to do with me?

They were living out their own lives
in my head—; *they had nothing to do with me!*

It started again.

I kept telling myself not to be frightened; but I
couldn't get it to stop.
                    I kept telling myself, "Wait,
it will go away. It's bound to stop soon.
It's only a drug!"

But I believed it would never end—
the roller coaster; the blood; the clouds;
the words; the tunnel . . .

I thought: "This is what it must be like
to be crazy!"

. . . and waited for it to stop.

3

I was having lunch in the diner
near the library
when I started to hear voices.

Not like the voices you hear
when you're trying to write something, and you
hear the words you're going to write.

I thought someone was *talking* to me.
I even looked around.
No one was there.

They were familiar voices, voices
I could almost identify . . .
pleasant, soothing voices. I thought,

"Am I crazy?
This is what it must be like
to be crazy."

But I was certain I wasn't crazy.
I could think perfectly straight. I was
aware of what was happening.

Everything made sense.

•

The voices told me to
avoid the person sitting at the counter
who didn't like me; and go home.

They suggested I clean my apartment
(which was a mess). I immediately
started putting things in order.

Stacks of papers and books.
All my notes. I arranged them
by language; then by author.

I worked all night
and all the next morning and afternoon.
The voices encouraged me. They

seemed pleased. I stayed awake three days!
(They let me eat, but made me
throw out any food I didn't finish.)

Before I finally fell asleep, they
told me to call the man at the diner—
tell him I knew what he was up to, and that

it wouldn't do him any good.
I called him—he wasn't home. Then
slept a couple of hours . . .

When I woke up, the voices were
still there.
They were in my dreams.

They woke me up.

•

They told me to go out, see a movie.
I forget what I saw—a foreign film. I watched it
over and over, till the theater closed.

I went back to the diner, *starving.*
All through my sandwich, the voices
decided what I should do next.

Burn all my photographs; smash
the mirror; disconnect the telephone;
move! . . . I was lucky,

the next day I found a smaller apartment
in the same building.
A week later I was moved in.

I took only what I needed:
mattress, kitchen table, books.
And my notes—which they made me put

into another new order.

I read Greek tragedies, and
saw a lot of movies the next few months.
I avoided people.

Before the phone was disconnected, I
called the man at the diner—warning him
that I was disconnecting my phone.

He knocked at my door once.
I didn't answer.
They wouldn't let me.

I was sleeping
two hours a night. I
couldn't eat.

I stopped going out.

·

All at once, I was overwhelmed by a
terrible black cloud. I was
suffocating. I didn't know how to get out.

I got very scared.

The voices got angry with me. They began
hammering at me that I
didn't deserve to live.

I didn't know what to do—
I was convinced
they were right.

I didn't "do" anything. I would
just lie there—sweating and shivering,
thinking I should die.

I didn't *want* to die. I wanted
to see a doctor.
They wouldn't let me.

They kept getting louder. And
angrier with me.
Then suddenly, they turned

on each other . . . They started
disagreeing. Violently.
There were bitter arguments.

In a strange language. *I couldn't understand
the words*. My head
was aching. The noise was unbearable.

THEY WERE TEARING ME APART.

·

I had to get away. Apparently,
I took a bus to Canada.
In Montreal, I was arrested.

I was apparently
walking the streets all night,
yelling obscenities.

My mother had me
transferred to the hospital
here.

It's all a blur.

·

Even in the hospital, drugged,
I could hear them.
They told me to brush my teeth.

I can still hear them.

Sometimes they're so mild, I'm not sure
if they're there or not—
my own breathing drowns them out.

When I stop taking
the drug,
they go wild—screaming at me to

kill myself! throw myself
through the window!
Twice, recently, they predicted

someone was going to die . . .

I've aged. My joints ache.
My hair is falling out.
The drug makes me talk funny.

I don't have any friends.

It's finally sinking in
that I'm not supposed to be
"hearing Voices" . . .

that they're *not separate* from ME.

The doctors tell me they
don't know what else they can do.
Nobody seems to know

why this happened to me.
They say there's
"no guarantee"

I will ever completely recover.

4

the ability of her mind to create
the ability of her mind to control
her capacity to be
whatever she tried to be

My girlfriend's sister had unique talents;
the most remarkable was that she
used to sing us
the "Hallelujah" Chorus—
all four voices, simultaneously.

She could add up all the numbers
of my telephone number, to tell
my future—she lived in
the fourth dimension,
where she learned how to count and spell.

She left home to go to college,
how could she have come to harm?
We were shocked—and bewildered—
when we first heard
that she was "cutting holes in her arm."

I visited her in the hospital.
It was difficult to look.
She was bandaged; and dizzy
from daily shock-therapy;
and fat from the drugs she took.

She spoke easily; her animation
concealed my embarrassment.
But her eyes, in the gaps
in our gossip,
revealed painful, profound discontent.

> *the inability of her mind to accept*
> *the inability of her mind to endure*
> *her desperate wish to be*
> *what she could only try to be*

After years of recoveries and relapses,
she is beautiful—thin and strong.
The diagnoses had been
mistaken:
there was nothing "mentally" wrong.

It was only chemistry; only
the body affecting the brain.
The reasons for losing
one's mind are confusing—
her treatments were, literally, insane.

Now she works in California—
Chief Computer-Programmer.
She lives mainly in
three dimensions;
the past is mainly a blur.

She flies east to see her sister
on her annual business trips.
Her sense of irony
is her refinery
transmuting Melancholy and Rage into quips.

She eats what the doctors tell her—
it's a very narrow list.
Some of the scars
have disappeared.
Some of the symptoms persist.

the ability of her mind to accept
the ability of her mind to endure
her desire to be
what she doesn't have to be

On the Recent Deaths of His Friend Colonna and His Lady Laura

(from Petrarch)

Broken. The high column. The green laurel.
The shade in which my tired thoughts
could rest.
      I have lost what is, to retrieve,
hopeless; no matter where I look—no wind
can reach them, no ocean touch them.

You have taken away both my treasures,
Death. They made my life easy, my step high.
To restore them?
      Not earth or empire, not jewels, not even
money itself.

But since destiny has consented, what is left
if not to have a sad soul?
      to be constantly
on the edge of tears; head bent down.

Is this our life?
      It seems so lovely. But how easily we lose
in one morning, what took so many years to get
and such great pain.

The Recital

He sits there, staring into the keyboard—
baggy rented tux; sagging shoulders; limp hair
nearly brushing the keys—
                              hesitating to begin.

His eyes glazed, as if he'd been up a week
on Coca Cola and pills;
                              a Coke bottle (giant-size)
half-empty at the foot of the piano bench . . .

A few Music people; secretaries from
his lab; the two poets he had studied with;
and assorted friends
                              half-fill the small hall.

The recital is ambitious, demanding:
Romantic-ecstatic and jagged-Modern—sometimes
hard to tell apart in his playing;

frustrated by the almost willful refusal
of his fingers to deal with all the notes;

but riveting—certain that music has to "intend,"
and stopping at nothing
                              to intend *something* . . .

Encouraging applause: a crooked, self-
deprecating bow from the waist.

Intermission is a relief.

"Amazing piano playing . . . for a physicist."
"Why does he *do* this to himself?"
                              "He didn't
look happy . . ."
                    "What if he decides to play
the first half over again?"

Back inside, the conversational hum drops;
then grows . . .
                    Where is he? Still backstage?
Home? Dead? . . . The speculation is amused;

and dismayed.

Messages are sent; assurances returned.
Forty, fifty minutes . . . Nobody leaves;

no one is surprised.

Could he have done *anything* to
keep his suffering from the audience?

(How many in it had already
suffered with him his poems, jobs, addictions?)

Or is this his way of trying?

Sheepishly, he reappears . . . And begins.
No waiting.
                    His intensity—this time—
controlled by his intentions . . .

What does he have to go through—;
what process, *effort*, finally
allows him to go on?

And what defeats it?

He'd have a poem accepted by a national magazine,
using an image drawn from his experiments,—
only to withdraw it, out of fear he'd lose his job.

He'd change jobs. Move home.
And give up practicing; virtually
stop writing.

Then cancer . . . springing (he was sure)
from all the pills: making him go through
a surgical attempt to prolong his life . . .

He wanted time
to straighten himself out; to try to write more poems—

he had three months.

Dead before forty,
what brought him distinction

besides what already had?

> His astonishing diversity
> of unfulfilled talent;
>
> and the unrewarded
> diversity of his suffering.

Self-Portrait

for Ralph Hamilton

"I was sitting in her living room,
looking very hard at the painting I had given her.
I asked her for a knife, and very deliberately
cut up the canvas. She was furious;
I told her, 'I'll paint you a good one.'

—Every painting is a self-portrait.

I always
straighten the pictures on people's walls . . .

I live at home,
painting while my parents are away at work.
I cook their dinner. It's a compromise,
but it's the only way I can afford to work;
better to compromise
my life.
        And if I suffer—
so much the better; not
easy.

They're amazingly patient—
my mother thinks I'm a 'great artist.'
My paintings are all over the walls,
mostly piled up against the window
in the dining room. (The dining room
hasn't seen the light of day in three years.)

I read a lot, when I'm not painting,
and play the piano—badly.
I'm fascinated by words. Some of my paintings
have words in them: AWAY . . .
GET WELL. In college,
I wrote my autobiography.

I've been commissioned to do a portrait—
I've done several;

                    but I shouldn't do them,
I don't know how. Every portrait
becomes just another painting . . . "

In your self-portrait,
the blinds are open, but you are looking
away; your eyes green, and enormous.
There is a sunny street outside—
grey and black shadows cover your face; your mouth
twisted with irony, or tenderness,
refusing to speak.
You say, "It's just another painting."

—A train disappearing over a hill;
a burnt-out house; two trucks colliding
in mid-air;
                your father; your mother; a baby;
a chair; a hand on a venetian blind . . .
"Every painting is a self-portrait."

Apparitions

"On Christmas Eve, the 42nd Street Station
is deserted by 11 P.M.
                    I was there once, all alone, when
a girl appeared—wearing a long, shapeless grey nightgown;
barefoot; dishevelled, but not unattractive; walking
toward me down the platform.
                    As she walked shakily by, I saw
BELLEVUE . . . printed in blue on the back of the gown.
She kept on walking, toward the farthest end of the station;
I followed her from a distance, until my train came."

•

Aug. 31. Disasters all day long.
Bathroom flooded (by an overnight guest). Spilled milk
all over the stove. Telephone ringing
at an "inopportune" moment—
(later asked where I've been "all morning.")
A bulb burnt out; lines busy; no one home . . . What next?

Another year.

The summer's over—still no Ph.D., the book
unpublished, "relationships" in doubt . . .
"No day is over until it ends."

There have been better days.
Wrote sonnets; read Latin; played the violin—
Applause, Affection . . .

And worse. Injury. Severance. Divorce (no marriage).

Money, phone numbers, opportunities, ambitions—
"All is not lost; the day's not over yet."

•

"It was on Eighth Avenue in the late forties,—in broad daylight.
An Oriental lady, in a floppy, cream-colored picture hat, lacy

white gloves, and white dress: up to her neck in spirals of
white organdy—sitting, with her hands folded primly in her lap,
in a rickshaw; pulled slowly through the Eighth Avenue traffic
by a huge black man, with bare feet and no shirt."

•

Nov. 27. Third awful party in three months.
Cruisy, boozy, fragments of our host's "past"—
caviar (distinctly lower case), devilled
eggs, vomiting drunks.
Not as bad as the other two . . . maybe
it was just me.

October? Death . . .
movie-set apartment—nobody moving.
GRAND OPENING: Important
people ("Hi, who are YOU?"), plants, artists—
early departure.

September on Nantucket: desperate
last-minute weekenders. R.X. sliding
off the wagon; B.A. groping; M.P. regaining
considerable articulateness, after last year's stroke.
—Interminable politics (the Jews and the Irish); local
changes; their tales

of strange "appearances" in New York City . . .

•

"Late for work, late one morning, on the subway
to Queens (still in my twenties),
                                        I was sitting opposite
an old woman, who was leaning forward, and swaying
over the fingers of her left hand, which she held up
close to herself—and seemed to be counting, one at a time,
with each corresponding finger of her right hand.
She looked up at me, and motioned me to come over to her;
I did. She leaned over to whisper in my ear:
'Ich bin krank.'

She rested her head in my lap.
I put my arm around her; people began to look away . . .
I called to a guard. When the train stopped, we carried her onto the platform—

                  where she died. We waited
until the police came and took her body away."